# The Mixology Connoisseur's Guide To Cocktails

By
Hassett Gravois

This book is dedicated with love to those of you that supported me and my craziest ideas, you know who you are. Love you! xoxo

This small guide is to help you learn how to Mix and impress your friends with classic and specialty drinks!

I have chosen a few of the most popular and traditional drinks as well as some unique ones, (and need to know) bar terms and some other useful information. (I've Even included a few blank pages in the back for some of your own notes.)

# Mint Julep

What you need:

- Mint Leaves
- ½ oz Simple Syrup
- 2 ½ oz Bourbon
- Mint Sprig for garnish

Add Mint and simple syrup into a Highball glass and Muddle (until it becomes a paste be sure to leave bits of leaf in it) fill with crushed ice then add bourbon and stir.

**\*Did you know:** The Mint Julep's original purpose was Medicinal (a protective against Malaria) but now is commonly associated (and served) at the Kentucky Derby.

# Long Island Iced Tea

- ¾ oz Tequila

- ¾ oz Vodka

- ¾ oz Triple Sec

- ¾ oz Gin

- ¾ oz Light Rum

- 1 oz Sour Mix

- Cola

Combine the ingredients over ice in a highball glass add cola for color garnish with a lemon wedge & stir stick

*Did you know: Long Island Iced Tea really has nothing to do with iced tea it's just a name so you don't look like a drunk when you order this at a 3 PM meeting!

# Dirty Martini

- 2 oz Vodka or Gin
- 2/3 oz Dry Vermouth
- 2/3 Oz Olive Brine
- 2 Olives

Shake over cracked ice and strain into a cocktail glass and garnish with 2 olives.

**You can find "Dirty Martini Mix" or just strain some of the brine from the olives you are using to garnish

"Vodka Cures all" – **Storm DuBois**

# Cosmopolitan

- 1 1/2 oz Vodka
- 1/4 oz Triple Sec
- 1/4 oz Lime Juice
- 1/4 oz Cranberry juice

Shake with ice and strain into a chilled cocktail glass garnish with a lime wedge.

**Note:** Some people like to garnish with lemon or lime twists (sometimes even make a flag with a cherry and a lime wedge)

"Here's to alcohol, the rose colored glasses of life."-**F. Scott Fitzgerald**

# A.M.F.

- 1/2 Oz Vodka

- 1/2 Oz Rum

- 1/2 oz Tequila

- 1/2 oz Gin

- 1/2 oz Blue Curacao

- 2 oz Sweet & Sour Mix

- 2 oz Lemon lime Soda

Pour all ingredients into a highball glass partially filled with ice stir and top with soda.

**\*Did you know:** Distilled spirits like ginger wine, vodka, absinthe, whiskey, brandy, rum, tequila and gin contain no carbohydrates, no fats of any kind, and no cholesterol.

# Imperial Fizz

- ½ oz White Rum
- 1 ½ oz Whiskey
- 1 oz Lemon Juice
- 1 tsp Powdered Sugar
- Carbonated Water
- Lemon Wedge

Shake rum, whiskey, lemon juice, and powdered sugar together pour into a highball glass partially filled with ice add carbonated water and serve. Garnish with a lemon wedge.

**Note:** partially filling a glass is usually best to fill it about ¾ as opposed as to the top (with ice)

# Old Fashioned

- ½ Teaspoon Sugar
- 3 dashes of Bitters
- Club soda
- 2oz bourbon whiskey

Add sugar, 3 dashes  Bitters and a tiny splash of club soda crush the sugar and muddle (meanwhile rotating the glass) Add Ice cubes pour whiskey add cherry serve with a stir stick.

"My speech isn't slurred I'm just talking in cursive." - **Unknown**

# Manhattan

- 1/2 oz Sweet Vermouth
- 2 oz Whiskey
- 1 Dash Angostura Bitters

Add all ingredients into a shaker with ice and strain into a chilled martini glass ; garnish with a cherry.

*Did you know: Sir Winston Churchill was one of the world's heaviest drinkers

"I have taken more out of alcohol than alcohol has taken out of me."

-Winston Churchill

# Bourbon & Water

One of the simplest drinks you could make!

- 2 oz Bourbon
- Water

Fill a highball glass with ice, pour bourbon and top with water.

# Bourbon Neat:

- Bourbon

Pour Bourbon & Serve into a rocks glass.

**\*Did you know:** In 1964, Congress declared Bourbon to be the official spirit of the United States it takes the name from Bourbon County in Kentucky.

# Cape Codder:

- 2 Oz. Vodka

- 2 oz Cranberry Juice

- ½ Oz Lime Juice

Pour Vodka, Cranberry juice and lime juice in a shaker with ice pour, into a highball glass. Garnish with a lime wedge or wheel.

**Note:** You can make this a fizzy drink by topping with soda water.

**\*Did you know:** The Cape codder is commonly used to help cure Bladder/Urinary Tract infections.

# B&B

- ¾ Oz Brandy
- ¾ Oz Benedictine

Float brandy over Benedictine in a shot glass.

# Gin & Tonic

- 2 oz Gin
- Tonic Water

Pour Gin into an Ice filled highball glass top with tonic water Garnish with a lime wedge.

"Once, during Prohibition, I was forced to live for days on nothing but food and water." **-W.C. Fields**

# Rum & Coke

- 1 ¼ oz Dark Rum
- 6 oz Coke

In a highball glass filled with ice pour rum then add coke and stir. Garnish with a lemon wedge

Did you know: This beverage is also called a 'Cuba Libre' in celebration of the newly freed Cuba. However the exact origin of this beverage is still a mystery.

# Scotch & Soda

- 1 ½ oz Scotch
- Club soda

In a rocks glass pour scotch then fill with (chilled) club soda and Garnish with a Lemon twist.

# Screwdriver

- 1 ½ oz Vodka
- 5 oz Orange Juice

Add Vodka and Orange Juice to an ice filled highball glass and stir. Garnish with an orange slice.

## Americano:

- 2oz Campari
- 2oz Bianco Vermouth
- Club Soda

Pour Campari and Bianco Vermouth into an ice filled highball glass, then fill with club soda and stir garnish with a slice of orange.

# Tequila Sunrise

- 2 oz Tequila

- 4 oz Orange Juice

- ¾ oz Grenadine

- 2 Cherries

Shake Tequila and Orange Juice into an ice filled Highball Glass add cherries then slowly pour grenadine over the top

**Note:** Usually the drinker stirs the drink to mix in the grenadine you can stir the tequila and Orange juice to evenly distribute the flavor then top with grenadine.

"Candy Is dandy, But liquor Is quicker."
**-Ogden Nash**

# Pink Squirrel

- 1 tbsp White crème de cacao
- 1oz crème de Noyeaux
- 1 tbsp light cream

Shake with ice and strain into a chilled cocktail glass

# Jager Bomb:

- 1 oz Jagermeister
- ½ can Red bull Energy Drink

Pour the Red Bull into a pint glass and drop the shot glass full of Jagermeister into the pint glass and Drink fast!

"Everybody should believe in something; I believe I'll have another drink." - **Unknown**

# Rob Roy

- ¾ oz Sweet Vermouth
- 1 ½ oz Scotch

Shake with ice and serve in a martini glass garnish with a cherry.

# Gimlet

- 2 oz Gin
- 1 3/4 oz Lime juice

Shake Gin & Lime Juice with ice strain into a chilled martini glass.

"Something about today makes me want to be hung over tomorrow." - **Unknown**

# Original Slippery Nipple

- ½ oz Bailey's Irish Cream
- ½ oz Preach Schnapps

Mix and serve in a shot glass.

# Slippery Nipple

- ½ oz irish cream
- ½ oz sambuca

Layer in a shot glass

She has many rare and charming qualities, but sobriety is not one of them. **-Jane Austen**

# Mojito:

- 2oz white rum
- Soda water
- 2tsp sugar
- 1 lime
- 4 mint leaves

Muddle sugar mint and lime into a highball glass add rum then stir and fill with ice Top with club soda and garnish with a lime and mint sprig.

"My speech isn't slurred I'm just talking in cursive." **- Unknown**

# John Collins

- 2 oz bourbon
- 1oz Lemon Juice
- 3oz club soda
- 1tsp fine sugar

Shake bourbon, lemon juice and sugar then strain into an ice filled highball glass, add club soda then stir garnish with a cherry and an orange slice.

## FU

- 1 1/2 oz Frangelico
- 2 1/4 oz Lemon-lime soda

Pour over ice into a rocks glass.

# Godfather

- 3/4 oz Amaretto
- 1 1/2 oz Scotch

Pour ingredients over ice in a rocks glass. Add cherry and serve.

# Tom Collins

- 2 oz Gin
- 1 oz Lemon Juice
- club soda
- 1tsp fine sugar

Shake lemon juice gin and sugar with ice and strain in a highball glass (partially filled with ice) add the club soda, stir then garnish with a cherry and an orange slice.

# Sidecar

- 2oz Cognac
- 1oz Cointreau
- 1oz lemon juice

Shake with cracked ice and serve in a chilled cocktail glass.

# Mimosa

- 4oz Champagne
- 1oz Orange Juice

Pour orange juice into champagne flute then SLOWLY add champagne garnish with an orange wheel or slice.

(It's ok to add more juice and a little less liquor or equal parts based on personal preference)

# Bloody Mary

- 2 oz vodka
- 3oz tomato juice
- ½ tsp Worcestershire sauce
- 2 dashes of Tabasco sauce
- 1 dash pepper
- 1 dash celery salt
- ½ horseradish

Shake with ice and strain into an ice filled highball glass garnish with a celery stalk.

** To make this into a **Bloody Caesar** replace the tomato juice with Clamato juice or add a splash of Clam Juice.

Take me down to the bar! We'll drink breakfast together! - **W.C. Fields**

# Bloody Maria

- 1 oz Tequila
- 1 dash lemon juice
- 2oz tomato juice
- 1dash Tabasco sauce
- 1 dash celery salt

Shake with ice and strain into an ice filled rocks glass garnish with a slice of lemon

**Did you know** :People who drink in moderation tend to be healthier and live longer than those who either abstain or abuse alcohol.

# Gin Sling

- 2oz gin
- 1tsp water
- 1oz lemon juice
- 1tsp powdered sugar

(Disolve sugar with water and lemon juice) then add gin pour in a rocks glass filled with ice garnish with an orange twist.

# Dry Martini

- 1 2/3 oz Gin
- 1/3 oz Dry Vermouth

Shake with ice and strain into a chilled martini glass garnish with an olive.

# Mai Tai

- 1 oz light rum
- 1oz gold rum
- 1oz dark rum
- ½ Orange Curaco
- ½ oz lime juice
- ½ oz Orgeat syrup

Shake all the ingredients except the dark rum, strain into a chilled rocks glass top with the dark rum garnish with a cherry.

"If you keep on drinking rum, the world will soon be quit of a very dirty scoundrel.
**-Robert Louis Stevenson**

# Gibson

- 4oz Gin
- 1/2 Dry Vermouth

Stir with ice strain into a martini glass garnish with onions.

**a Gibson is almost the same as a dry martini except served with cocktail onions and stirred. (shaken is optional)

## Apple Martini

- 1/2 oz Apple schnapps
- 1/2 Gin

Shake with ice and strain into a martini glass.

# Vodka Collins

- 2 oz Vodka
- 1oz Lemon Juice
- club soda
- 1 tsp powdered sugar

Shake lemon juice, sugar and vodka with ice strain into a chilled highball glass. Add some ice, fill with club soda then stir and garnish with lemon ,orange slices and a cherry.

# Tabuie

- 1 oz Drambuie
- 1 oz Tuaca

Chill and strain into a shot glass.

(Tuaca is an Italian sweet liqueur, flavoured with cirtus.)

# Sex On The Beach

- ½ oz  apple schnapps
- ½ oz peach schnapps
- ½ oz cranberry juice
- ½ pineapple juice

Shake with ice and strain into a highball glass.

# Sea Breeze

- 1 3/4 oz Vodka
- 3 oz Cranberry juice
- 1 oz Grapefruit juice

Shake the cranberry and vodka juice pour over ice into a highball glass filled with ice top with grapefruit juice and garnish with a slice of grapefruit.

# Rum Runner

- 1 oz  white rum
- ¼ oz crème de banane
- ¼ oz cherry brandy
- ½ Bacardi 151 proof rum
- ½ oz grenadine
- 3oz pina colada mix

blend with ice and pour into a cocktail glass top with the Bacardi 151

Always do sober what you said you'd do drunk. That will teach you to keep your mouth shut. – Ernest Hemingway

# Lemon Drop

- 1 1/2 Oz Vodka
- 1/2 oz Triple Sec
- 1 tsp sugar

Shake all ingredients over ice and strain into a cocktail glass, sugar the rim and garnish with a lemon slice or lemon twist.

# Grape ape

- 1 1/2 oz Grape Pucker
- 1 oz Vodka
- Splash of lime soda
- Splash of soda water

Shake and pour into a cocktail glass top with lime soda and soda water.

# Black Russian

- 1/2 Oz Vodka
- 3/4 Oz Coffee Liqueur

Pour over ice into a rocks glass.

# White Russian

- 2 oz Vodka
- 1 oz Coffee Liqueur
- 3/4 oz Half & Half

Pour the vodka and coffee liqueur into a rocks glass filled with ice top with Half & Half.

# Texas Style Mexican Martini

- 1oz Tequila Silver
- 1/4oz Grand Marnier
- 3oz Sour Mix
- 1 oz Lime juice
- 1oz Orange Juice
- Olives

Shake with ice strain into a salted martini glass serve with olives

**Did you know**: People who drink in moderation tend to be healthier and live longer than those who either abstain or abuse alcohol.

# Tequila Sunrise

- 2 oz Tequila
- 4oz Orange Juice
- 3/4 Grenadine

Shake tequila and orange juice, then strain into an ice filled highball glass. Top with grenadine and let settle. Garnish with a cherry then stir before drinking.

# Tequila Sunset

- 2oz Tequila
- 3/4 Blackberry Brandy
- 4 oz Orange juice

Shake tequila and orange juice, strain into an ice filled highball glass and top with blackberry brandy. Garnish with a cherry.

# Haiku

- 2 oz Sake
- Sash of dry vermouth

Shake and strain into a rocks glass garnish with a cocktail onion.

# G & T (Gin & Tonic)

- 2 oz Gin
- Tonic Water

Pour gin into an ice filled highball glass and fill with tonic water stir and garnish with a lime wedge.

I may be drunk, but in the morning I'll be sober and you'll still be ugly. – Winston Churchill

## Azza

- 1/2 oz Malibu Rum
- 1/2 Peach Schnapps

Pour into a shot glass.

## Woo-Hoo

- 1/3 oz Frangelico
- 1/3 oz Kahlua
- 1/3 oz Milk

Shake with ice and strain into a martini glass.

Being half drunk is just another way of saying 'You're almost there.' – **Jarrod Conway**

# Tainted Love

- 2oz Whiskey
- 4oz Root Beer

Mix over ice and strain into a cocktail glass.

# Heroin

- 1/2 oz Grand Marnier
- 1/2 Oz Sambuca

Layer in a shot glass.

I feel sorry for people who don't drink. They wake up in the morning and that's the best they're going to feel all day. **– Frank Sinatra**

# Blue Moon

- 3/4 oz Blue Curacao
- 1 1/2 oz Gin

Shake with ice and strain into a chilled cocktail glass, garnish with a lemon twist.

# Flash Back

- 3oz Vodka
- 5oz Gatorade
- Ginger ale

Shake Gatorade and Vodka & strain into an ice filled highball glass then fill with ginger ale.

"Drunkenness is nothing but voluntary madness" -**Seneca**

# Absinthe Sour

- 1/4 oz Absinthe
- 3/4 oz Lemon Juice
- 1/2 tbsp sugar

Shake with ice then strain into a shot glass.

# Acid Rain

- 1/3 oz Curacao
- 1/2 oz Irish Cream
- 1/3 Oz Triple Sec

Combine Curacao and triple sec into a shooter glass, then add Irish cream to top up (wait until it becomes one color) then shoot!

# Reference Guide

# Key Terms

These are a few need to know terms (just the basics) to help make this easier! Some of them being more difficult than others to remember! Don't worry you'll get it!

**Blend** - The combining or mixing of liquors.

**Bruised**: A "**straight up**" Martini that is shaken, instead of stirred

**Call Drink:** A cocktail made with a brand name liquor

**Chaser:** A beverage drank immediately after a shot of liquor to eliminate the flavor and cleanse the palate.

**Cooler** A drink consisting of ginger ale, soda water, and a fresh spiral or twist of citrus fruit rind, served in a Collins or highball glass.

**Dash/Splash** - The smallest bar measurement.

**Double**: A drink with double the amount of liquor.

**Frappé /Mist**: A drink poured over crushed ice.

**Float** - A small amount of liquor poured carefully so that it floats on a drink.

**Lace** - Normally applies to the last ingredient in a recipe, meaning to pour onto the top of the drink.

**Mexican Style/Electric:** A drink with Tequila poured on top means the drink prepared as usual, but topped off with (extra) Tequila.

**Modifier** - A different ingredient in cocktails.

**Muddle:** To crush or grind with a mortar and pestle to release flavors.

**Neat/Plain:** Served straight, without mixers, ice, or other additives.

**Nightcap** A wine or liquor taken before bedtime.

**On the Rocks**: A drink served over cubed ice (Rocks meaning Ice)

**Proof -** An American system for measuring alcohol content by volume. Half the alcohol content.

**Punch:** A large batch cocktail mixed in a bowl. Punches usually consist of one or more liquors along with various mixers such as juice, soda, or even wine.

**Screaming**: A drink prepared as usual but topped with extra vodka

**(With a) Squeeze**: A lime "squeezed" on top of the drink and dropped into it

**Shake:** A method of mixing drink ingredients, usually with ice to chill at the same time.

**Shot:** A typical bar unit of measure equaling 1.5 ounces.

**Simple Syrup:** A syrup made of sugar and water used to sweeten drinks.

**Sour:** A cocktail made with a liquor, lemon or lime juice, and sugar (or pre-made sour mix).

**Sparkling:** Carbonated.

**Straight Up:** The ingredients of the drink are chilled before they are poured into the serving glass. No ice! A drink served **neat** without ice

**Toddy:** Hot water, lemon, and liquor (usually whiskey or bourbon).

**Topless**: A Margarita with a salt less rim.

**Top Off:** Filling the glass the rest of the way with the specified liquid (e.g. top off with soda).

**(With a)Twist:** Served with a small amount of citrus squeezed into the drink.


**Virgin/Unleaded:** A cocktail or other drink made without alcohol.


**Well Drink:** A liquor and mixer, of which neither are defined brands. (Generic)


**Wet**: More of the mix- Example a wet rum and coke- meaning use less rum and more coke


**Zest** - A small piece of the colored part of a lemon or orange peel

# Measurement Guide

This is just a small reference guide with the measurements

1 Teaspoon or Bar Spoon = 1/8 oz

1 Tablespoon=3/8 oz

1 Pony= 1oz

1 Jigger 1-1/2 oz

1 wineglass=4 oz

1 split = 6oz

1 cup = 8oz

Have you seen the measurement 'cl'? It means Centiliter, which is approximately 1 shot (1oz)

# Glassware

**Beer mug** : The traditional beer container.  Usually 16 oz. Often placed in the freezer to help keep the beer colder longer!

**Brandy Snifter:**  The shape of this glass concentrates the alcoholic smells to the top of the glass as your hands warm the brandy usually about 17-18 oz.

**Champagne Flute:** This glass is designed to show off the waltzing bubbles usually 6 oz.

**Cocktail Glass/Martini Glass:**  This glass has a triangle shaped with a long stem. Between  4-12 oz.

**Highball glass**  A straight-sided glass, used for mixer combined drinks  and those served on rocks. Between: 8-12 oz.

**Margarita glass** a slightly larger and more rounded than a cocktail glass with a broad-rim for holding salt, It is also used in daiquiris and other fruit drinks. About 12 oz.

**Rocks/Old-fashioned glass :** A short, round glass, suitable for cocktails or liquor served on the rocks, or neat. Between: 8-10 oz.

**Pilsner:** Tall, slender and tapered. The slender glass will reveal the color and carbonation of the beer, and the broad top will help maintain a beer head.

**Punch bowl:** A large bowl used for punches or large mixes. Between 1-5 gallons.

**Red wine glass:** A clear, thin, stemmed glass with a round bowl tapering inward at the rim. The glass is 8 oz however

**Shot glass**: Is a small glass made of thick glass designed to hold between 1 – 1 ½ oz of liquor.

# Liquor Abbreviations (Well)

Bourbon - B/
Brandy - BR/
Gin-G/
Scotch-S/
Tequila-T/
Vodka-V/

Pretty easy to remember: It's the first
letter with the exception
of Brandy which is the first 2!

# Your Notes:

Don't forget to find us online on Facebook, and Twitter.

www.MixologyConnoisseur.com

@MixologyExpert

www.ingramcontent.com/pod-product-compliance
Lightning Source LLC
Chambersburg PA
CBHW032035090426
42741CB00006B/830